Table of Contents

Can you find these words?

cement

electrician

plumber

tiles

Building a House

We can build a house.

We get **cement**.

cement

We use it to make the floor.

We get wood.

We build the walls.

We add windows.

We add doors.

A **plumber** places pipes for water.

plumber

An **electrician** wires the lights.

electrician

We put **tiles** on the roof.

tiles

We paint the house.

Did you find these words?

We get **cement**.

An **electrician** wires the lights.

A **plumber** places pipes for water.

We put **tiles** on the roof.

Photo Glossary

 **cement** (suh-MENT): A fine powder that gets hard when mixed with water and makes concrete.

 **electrician** (i-lek-TRISH-uhn): A person who installs or fixes electrical equipment.

 **plumber** (PLUHM-ur): A person who installs or repairs pipes so people can have water in a home.

 **tiles** (tiles): Squares made of stone, clay, or plastic that are used to make roofs.

Index

About the Author

Terri Fields likes reading with and writing for children. When she's not reading or writing, she likes walking on the beach.

© 2019 Rourke Educational Media

www.rourkeeducationalmedia.com

PHOTO CREDITS: Cover: ©EvgeniiAnd; p. 2,4,14,15: ©Christina Richards; p. 2,11,14,15: ©XiXinXing; p. 2,10,14,15: ©Phovoir; p. 2,12,14,15: ©Terry J Alcorn; p. 3: ©kali9; p. 5: ©Brian Chase; p. 6: ©fstop123; p. 8: ©?David Sacks; p. 9: ©artursfoto; p. 13: ©Feverpitched.

Edited by: Keli Sipperley
Cover design by: Kathy Walsh
Interior design by: Rhea Magaro-Wallace

Library of Congress PCN Data
Building a House / Terri Fields
(Discovery Days)
ISBN (hard cover)(alk. paper) 978-1-64156-177-8
ISBN (soft cover) 978-1-64156-233-1
ISBN (e-Book) 978-1-64156-285-0
Library of Congress Control Number: 2017957786

Printed in the United States of America, North Mankato, Minnesota